US Airstrikes in Syria: The Retaliatory Attack On Iranian IRGC and Affiliates

By

Gregory D. Richardson

Copyright

All rights reserved. No part of this publication may be reproduced, distributed, or transmitted in any form or by any means, including photocopying, recording, or other electronic or mechanical methods, without the prior written permission of the publisher, except in the case of brief quotations embodied in critical reviews and certain other noncommercial uses permitted by copyright law.

Copyright © Gregory D. Richardson, 2023.

Table of Contents

Chapter 1: US Hits Targets in Syria After Drone Kills US worker

Chapter 2: New Assault on a US Base in Syria

Chapter 1: US Hits Targets in Syria After Drone Kills US worker

The Pentagon said that a suspected Iranian-made drone struck northeast Syria on Thursday, killing a U.S. contractor and injuring five American service members and a second contractor. After this, US troops claimed to have carried out "precise airstrikes" in Syria on sites utilized by the Iranian Revolutionary Guard, killing at least four individuals, according to activist groups.

The act and the US response pose a danger to recent attempts to defuse tensions in the broader Middle East, where competing countries have made progress toward détente in recent days after years of unrest.

In a statement, U.S. Defense Secretary Lloyd Austin claimed that the country of origin of the drone was Iran, although he provided no additional quick proof to back up this assertion.

"The airstrikes were carried out in reaction to today's incident as well as a series of previous attacks against coalition troops in Syria," Austin said. These attacks were carried out by organizations connected to the Revolutionary Guard.

Iran uses a network of proxies around the Middle East to fight the U.S. and Israel, its main adversaries in the area.

According to the Pentagon, three more injured service members and the injured contractor were sent to medical facilities in Iraq, while two of the injured servicemen were treated locally.

Videos posted on social media overnight claimed to show explosions in Deir el-Zour, a vital area of Syria that borders Iraq and has oil deposits. The Syrian army and militia groups supported by Iran are in charge of the region, which has also recently been the focus of claimed Israeli bombings aimed against Iranian supply channels.

Iran and Syria's representatives at the United Nations in New York did not immediately recognize the attacks or react to calls for comment from The Associated Press.

Four persons were reported dead as a result of the US attacks, according to the activist organization Deir Ezzor 24. The attacks reportedly impacted the city of Deir el-Zour as well as militia sites close to Mayadeen and Boukamal, according to Deir Ezzor 24, which monitors news in the Deir el-Zour governorate. It claimed that civilians, including Iraqis, were hurt in the attacks.

Six Iranian-backed militants were killed at an armaments stockpile in the Harabesh area of Deir el-Zour, according to the Syrian Observatory for Human Rights, an opposition war monitor. Two fighters were reportedly killed by US bombardment at a checkpoint close to the town of Mayadeen, according to the Observatory, which depends on a network of local sources in Syria.

Another three fighters were killed in a second US attack that targeted a military outpost close to the town of Boukamal along the Iraqi border, according to the Observatory.

The paramilitary Revolutionary Guard of Iran, which reports directly to Ayatollah Ali Khamenei, the country's supreme leader, has been accused of conducting drone assaults throughout the larger Middle East.

As part of its campaign against Kiev, Moscow has recently started using Iranian drones in its assaults on targets around Ukraine. While Western countries and analysts have linked parts of the drones to Tehran, Iran has made several contradictory denials on the use of its drones in the battle.

While attempting to reopen their embassies in one other's nations, Saudi Arabia and Iran exchanged attacks. The kingdom also recognized plans to restore a Saudi consulate in Syria, where Iran has long supported Bashar Assad, the country's beleaguered president, in the long-running conflict there.

The commander of the US military's Central Command, U.S. Army Gen. Michael "Erik" Kurilla, cautioned that American troops may launch more attacks if necessary. In a statement, Kurilla said that "we are prepared for scalable alternatives in the case of any more Iranian strikes."

Kurilla cautioned legislators that "Iran of today is vastly more militarily competent than it was even five years ago" when speaking before the U.S. House Armed Services Committee on Thursday. He referred to Iran's stockpile of drones and ballistic missiles.

Also, according to Kurilla, Iran has attacked US forces in Syria 78 times since January 2021.

Iran uses Iranian proxies as a cover tactic, according to Kurilla.

Around the strikes, it looked that diplomatic efforts to defuse the situation started right away. The U.S. national security advisor Jake Sullivan and Qatar's foreign minister spoke over the phone, according to Qatar's state-run news agency. With concerns over Tehran's nuclear program, Doha has lately served as a mediator between Iran and the U.S.

At about the same time, the foreign ministers of Qatar and Iran talked on the phone with Hossein Amirabdollahian.

Austin said that President Joseph Biden gave the go-ahead for the retaliation attacks.

Austin said: "We will always react at a time and location of our choice and, as President Biden has made plain, we will take any necessary actions to protect our people. "No faction will attack our soldiers without consequence."

Because of concerns with Iran, the U.S. previously attacked Syria under Biden's leadership. Biden launched assaults there in August 2022, February, and June 2021.

Although the exchange of strikes on Thursday comes at a delicate political time due to the "overall deterioration of U.S.-Iran relations and the stalling of the nuclear talks," Dareen Khalifa, a senior Syria analyst with the Brussels-based International Crisis Group, said she does not anticipate a significant escalation.

While she pointed out that they often do not result in fatalities, Khalifa added, "These tit-for-tat attacks have been going on for a long time."

The Biden administration, she said, "won't be eager to escalate in Syria now and will instead have a reasonably measured approach," even if "the possibility of an escalatory cycle is there.

To support coalition troops in their struggle against the Islamic State organization, US soldiers invaded Syria in 2015. The facility where the drone hit on Thursday took place, in northeastern Syria, is still under US maintenance. There are perhaps 900 US soldiers in Syria, including in the north and farther south and east, as well as many more contractors.

According to Hamidreza Azizi of the German Institute for International and Security Affairs, Iran has worked to "make life tough for U.S. soldiers stationed east of the Euphrates" since the U.S. drone attack that claimed the life of Revolutionary Guard Gen. Qassem Soleimani in 2020.

In a recent report, Azizi said that Iran "raised its backing for local proxies in Deir el-Zour while seeking to ally with the tribal groups in the region." "Due to the close vicinity, Iraqi factions also increased their activity along the Syrian border and in the region of Deir el-Zour."

The 2011 Arab Spring uprisings that roiled the Middle East as a whole and overthrew the governments of Egypt, Libya, Tunisia, and Yemen marked the beginning of the Syrian conflict. Later, it changed into a regional proxy war in which Assad is supported by both Russia and Iran.

According to the United Nations, the conflict has claimed the lives of nearly 300,000 people. These statistics do not reflect the troops and rebels lost in the war; it is estimated that there were thousands of them.

The threat of further American airstrikes "if necessary"

The commander of the US military's Central Command, U.S. Army Gen. Michael "Erik" Kurilla, cautioned that American troops may launch more attacks if necessary. In a statement, Kurilla said that "we are prepared for scalable alternatives in the case of any more Iranian strikes."

In addition, Iran has not yet responded to the attacks, which took place during the holy Muslim fasting month of Ramadan, according to Syria's state-run SANA news agency.

Kurilla said that Iran's drone fleet has grown to be "the greatest and most capable unmanned aerial vehicle force in the area" in a testimony before the House Armed Services Committee on Thursday.

Chapter 2: New Assault on a US Base in Syria

A day after a U.S. contractor was killed and five U.S. service personnel and another U.S. contractor were injured when a suspected Iranian drone bombed a facility on a coalition base in the same area, according to U.S. officials, a fresh missile attack targeted a U.S. post in northeast Syria on Friday.

There were "plenty of rockets" launched, according to U.S. authorities who verified the fresh assault on an American outpost on Friday. Nevertheless, no known U.S. injuries were reported.

A U.S. outpost close to the Al-Omar oil field in northeast Syria was said to have been the target of the Friday missile barrage, according to reports that first circulated.

The attack was originally reported by local media, including a pro-Iran site headquartered in Lebanon, and the Reuters news agency. Pictures and rumors on social media showed that at least one missile may have impacted nearby residences instead of its intended target.

The attack occurred just hours after U.S. Defense Secretary Lloyd Austin announced in a statement that U.S. Central Command forces had carried out "precision airstrikes" against locations in eastern Syria used by organizations linked to Iran's Revolutionary

Guard in retaliation for Thursday's deadly drone attack.

The unmanned aerial vehicle used in the strike on Thursday was identified as having Iranian origins by the intelligence community, according to the Defense Department.

According to the Pentagon, three more injured Americans and the injured contractor were sent to medical facilities in Iraq while two injured American service members were treated on the spot.

The US airstrikes on Thursday reportedly killed six militants with Iranian support at an armaments storage in Deir el-Zour, according to the Syrian Observatory for Human Rights, an opposition war monitor.

The U.S. also targeted an outpost close to the town of Mayadeen, according to the Observatory, which depends on a network of local contacts in Syria. This attack claimed the lives of two further fighters.

On Thursday, the Observatory said that a separate US airstrike had struck a military outpost close to the Iraqi border town of Boukamal.

Austin said that he had been directed by President Biden to carry out the retaliatory strikes. "The airstrikes were performed in reaction to today's incident as well as a series of previous attacks against Coalition troops in Syria," he stated.

Austin said: "We will always react at a time and location of our choice and, as President Biden has made plain, we will take any necessary actions to protect our people. "No faction will attack our soldiers without consequence."

According to Austin, "the United States took measured and deliberate action aimed at reducing the potential of escalation and minimizing deaths."

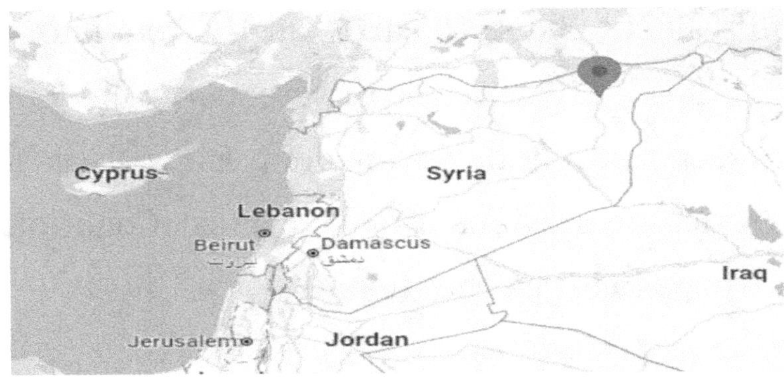

Source: Google Maps

The northeastern Syrian city of Hasakah is depicted on the map. According to the Pentagon, on March 23, 2023, an American contractor was killed and five American service members and another American contractor were injured by a suspected Iranian drone.

According to the Pentagon, the United States responded by conducting airstrikes on Syrian sites with ties to Iran.

As Saudi Arabia and Iran work to reopen embassies in each other's nations, the attack and U.S. response pose a threat to recent attempts to defuse tensions in the region.

The kingdom also acknowledged efforts to reopen its embassy in Syria, whose President Bashar Assad, who is under fire, has Iran's support in the protracted conflict in his nation.

The U.S. national security advisor Jake Sullivan and Qatar's foreign minister spoke over the phone, according to Qatar's state-run news agency. With concerns over Tehran's nuclear program, Doha has lately served as a mediator between Iran and the U.S.

At about the same time, the foreign ministers of Qatar and Iran talked on the phone with Hossein Amirabdollahian.

www.ingramcontent.com/pod-product-compliance
Lightning Source LLC
Chambersburg PA
CBHW071031260726
48662CB00024B/2334